Greater Than a Tourist Brosov Romania

50 Travel Tips from a Local

Alexandra Florea

Lock Haven, PA
All rights reserved.
ISBN: 9781521977286

> TOURIST

Alexandra Florea

BOOK DESCRIPTION

Are you excited about planning your next trip?

Do you want to try something new while traveling?

Would you like some guidance from a local?

If you answered yes to any of these questions, then this book is just for you.

Greater Than a Tourist –Brosov, Romania by Alexandra Florea offers the inside scope on Brosov. Most travel books tell you how to travel like a tourist. Although there's nothing wrong with that, as a part of the Greater than a Tourist series, this book will give you travel tips from someone who lives at your next travel destination.

In these pages you'll discover local advice that will help you throughout your stay. This book will not tell you exact addresses or store hours but instead will give you an excitement and knowledge from a local that you may not find in other smaller print travel books. Travel like a local. Slow down, stay in one place, and get to know the people and the culture of a place.

By the time you finish this book, you will be eager and prepared to travel to your next destination.

Alexandra Florea

TABLE OF CONTENTS

16. Shopping In Supermarkets

17. Shopping In Small Markets

18. Going To The Mall

19. Going Bowling Or Playing Pool

20. Visiting Museums

21. Visiting The Old Walls Of The City

22. Taking The Cable Car

23. Exercising

24. Visiting Belvedere Platform

25. Visiting The Black Church

26. Hanging Out In Council Square

27. Going To Poiana Brasov

28. Renting A Car

29. Parking Your Car

30. Traveling To Places Near By

31. Getting To Know The City

32. Getting Inspired

33. Taking Pictures

34. Speaking A Foreign Language

35. Speaking Romanian

36. Bounding With Locals

37. Looking For An Adventure

38. Swimming And Relaxation

39. Clubbing

DEDICATION

This book is dedicated to the wonderful people of Brasov whom express kindness to all tourists, to their free and open minded spirit.

I dedicate this book to Brasov as it would be an individual, to all it's beauty and rich history, as well as to all places touristic attractions part of county Brasov.

Alexandra Florea

ABOUT THE AUTHOR

Alexandra is originally from Bucharest, but every summer she is spending at least one month in Brasov. She loves renting apartments in alt houses near to Council Square because she feels in touch with local history.
During winter time she loves going to Brasov to practice winter sports and to fully enjoy the cold season.

Alexandra Florea

HOW TO USE THIS BOOK

This book was written by someone who has lived in an area for over three months. The author has made the best suggestions based on their own experiences in the area. Please check that these places are still available before traveling to the area. The goal of this book is to help travelers either dream or experience different locations by providing opinions from a local.

Alexandra Florea

FROM THE PUBLISHER

Traveling can be one of the most important moments in a person's life. The memories that you have of anticipating going somewhere new or getting to travel are some of the best. As a publisher of the Greater Than a Tourist book series, as well as the popular 50 Things to Know book series, we strive to help you learn about new places, spark your imagination, and inspire you.

Thought this book you will find something for every traveler. Wherever you are and whatever you do I wish you safe, fun, and inspiring travel.

Lisa Rusczyk Ed. D.
CZYK Publishing

Alexandra Florea

WELCOME TO > TOURIST

Alexandra Florea

INTRODUCTION

Brasov is one of the most visited cities in Romania due to it's rich history, geographic position and compelling rustic architecture.

Spending time here is fun and interesting. The city gives you a chance to bound with locals and other tourists. Everyone is so relaxed and the vibes are so chill, you get relaxed in no time just by feeling the cool vibe all around.

Every single day there is something to do in Brasov. There is no way you can get bored and times seem to pass really fast here. After one trip you will get addicted to this city and start planning for your return.

Tips were created to make your staying more enjoyable and to help each and every one of you find exactly what interests you and to smooth your journey.

Alexandra Florea

1. Booking Your Short Term House

I prefer booking a one room apartment, rather than the hotel.
When renting an apartment I get a unique home experience.
When getting the chance to leave in a big house with multiple
apartments, the experience relates with social bound.
Night in Brasov can be cold even during summer time, but
don't worry about it because hotels and hosts provide a
heating system that will take care of your need. Plus the
blankets are so soft and make the place more cozy and
comfortable.

2. Using Public Transportation

I usually use the bus to get from the train station to the center, or to travel around the city. The bus ticket with two ends (can be used twice) is 4 lei (Romanian currency) almost 1$. I always make sure to buy a few of them from the primary bus station outside the train station Brasov, but I also use the monthly pass.

Please make sure you have your ticket and that you have submitted it to the ticket machine inside the buss. From that moment the ticket is available for one hour.

This is important because every day there will be controllers that check every person for a ticket, and tourists are no exception.

3. Taking The Cab/Taxi

Cabs can be found in a line of order near train station, museums or basically the center of Brasov. I tend to use a cab when I'm in a hurry. A drive from the center to the train station is about 12-15 lei and that is about $3-4.

Cabs can be found standing in an line. Be aware, if your drive is 10 minutes away, the taxi driver might refuse to take you because serving you he is obliged to get back in line. For some of the taxi drivers that is an issue, that's why is better to ask them first if they are willing to take you to that address.

4. Finding a place to sleep

Brasov is manly known for massive amounts of tourists coming every single day. Even though there are more than three big hotels exactly in the center of Brasov and a few more all around, I recommend booking in advance.

If your trip to Brasov is unexpected and you really want to spend one night at the hotel, be prepared to spend between 400-900 lei (100-250$) for one room.

Compared to other cities in Romania when you can find people on the street offering keys for one night or more, in Brasov you will not encounter this situation.

5. Using A Credit Card

Most of restaurants, hotels, b&b and mini markets accept credit card payment.

The card must be VISA, MasterCard or Maestro. For other type of debit/credit card I recommend asking before deciding to dine, sleep or have a drink there.

When using booking.com please read the payment section and confirm before checking in.

Supermarkets accept credit card payment for the above listed types on credit/debit cards.

6. Using Cash

Cash is used in all facilities especially when going to the farmer's market, visiting castles or buying souvenirs.
I always find myself in need of something late into the night and non-stop shops only accept cash.

I recommend having small amounts of cash on you. Keep in mind what is necessary for the itinerary. The currency is called RON and is known by the name LEI.

Brasov is a safe city. I have never been robbed and never had heard about someone being in such a situation, but I also think that taking a precaution can make your staying more pleasant.

7. Going To The Bank

In Brasov are present all Romanian Banks, and their schedule is from 9 a.m. to 5 p.m. MoneyGram can be performed from any of those banks present and also WesternUnion by some of them.

I would not recommend cashing in a check performed by an institution that has no affiliation to Romania Banks due to the long amount of time spent on confirmation of all credentials. All bank personal speak English, so getting along will not be a problem. For any transaction that you're looking to have, your ID and passport are necessary.

8. Using The ATM

I usually use a the ATM when I'm preparing to go visit a castle or pay for the bus ticket. More than one ATM can be found in all parts of the city. ATM machines have video cameras inserted.

Before retrieving money, the bank will notify you about the commission in question and also the currency for that day. As for the type of credit/debit card in use, usually it shoul be VISA, MasterCard or Maestro. Feel free to ask the bank personal before trying to use a different type of credit/debit card.

9. Exchanging Foreign Currency

In Brasov foreign currency can be exchanged at the bank or at the exchange boutique. The main street that takes you to the Council Square (Piata Sfatului), named Republicii Street, has three exchange boutiques that usually offer a better exchange rate than the bank does.

As for ATM machines that offer foreign currency I can suggest using BCR, although I prefer making exchanges at exchange boutiques.

10. Stolling On Promenade Tampa

Promenade Tampa is one of my favorite places in Brasov. Near to the mountain, the air is fresh and the connection with nature is unique.

During springtime there is the risk of encountering bears and I suggest having a day walk, not a night one. Don't worry about the bears, they are not seen so often, maybe once or twice a year.

Strolling on Promenade Tampa can take you back to medieval times, as the old wall protecting the city from invaders is marking the path.

11. Encountering Bears

Bears can be seen in neighborhoods near to the mountains. If you see a small bear don't get near it, in stead try to go inside or find shelter because the the mama bear is close and she is dangerous.

When seeing any type of bear at a distance of 200 m I recommend keeping your calm and taking cover especially if the bear has not seen you.

Bears usually come down into those neighborhoods and night or bright morning because they know their can be food in the trash.
As I said in a previous chapter, bears are seen once or twice a year so don't worry about it, just keep in mind those small but eficient details.

12. Going Out For A Night Walk

I like going out on walks at dusk. At night time the city is very peaceful although might seem creepy without people on the street. Brasov is crowded during day time, but at night there are just a few persons on the street.

I would suggest walking along places you have passed by during the day like Republicii Street, Council Square or the neighborhood you have rented a place at.

13. Grabbing A Bite To Eat

Center of Brasov is my favorite place to eat, with lots of restaurants to choose from. Even if I want traditional food or Italian food, Republicii street is the place to be at.

My favorite place is called Ciucas Tavern and is on the right side of Hotel Coroana, where the food is amazing.
On Republicii Street there are a lot of pubs during summer time where you could eat a great salad or even pizza. All around the city there are great restaurants. When I want to eat at a new place I ask people on the street to make a suggestion.

14. Eating Traditional Food

Best traditional food I have ever had in Brasov is at Ciucas Tavern. The food is made with meat localy made as well as the drinks Ciucas made in the area. The prices are really good and the place is full at dinner time. Make sure to make a reservation if you're with a group and you want to have dinner there. For breakfast and lunch you don't need a reservation. For a great gastronomic experience I recommand the restaurant Gott by hotel Gott.

Feel free to check restrograf.ro for pictures of restaurants, their menu and opinions on food and staff.

15. Eating Fast Food

Sometimes I can have a carving for some fast food. KFC is right in the middle of Council Square. Good shaorma is hard to find in Brasov, but I don't really see the point for that when there are so many good restaurants where you could eat something much better.

As for McDonald's, you can find it at the entrance into Brasov if you're coming by car from Bucharest.
If you're more into pizza you should ask a local for advice, as I'm a fan of making my own pizza at home.

16. Shopping In Supermarkets

For those of us who like to spend more than one week in one place and also cook at home, the shooping is being done at a bit supermarket as Kaufland or Carrefour. Both can be found at the entrance into Brasov, if coming by car from Bucharest. Another Kaufland can be found at about 1 km from Old Town as known the center of Brasov.

Supermarkets are a great place to shop if you have rented a place for more than a week because the products are much more fresh than at a small mini market, and also the prices are reduced.

Best part about supermarkets is the fact that you can find anything you want from food to car accessories.

17. Shopping In Small Markets

I love going shopping at the farmer's market, 500 m from the Old Town, where the fruits and vegetables are fresh and organic.

I also enjoy the local man made cheese which has a unique taste and it's made by traditional means.

A small non-stop market can be found on Republicii Street in Old Town, but I only shop there on emergencies because the offer is a bit limited for my taste. In Brasov there are three Lidl shops where you can find more diversity. Other non-tops mini markets/shops can be found at every 500 -700 m from each other, but they only take cash.

18. Going To The Mall

When feeling the need to change the scenery I go to Magnolia Shopping Center, about 600 m from Old Town. Other malls and shopping centers can be found in Brasov, like Eliana Mall or Coresi Shopping Center, a bit far from Old Town, but with bus and taxi access. You can find stores like ZARA and H&M if you're interested in buying something casual. I recommend entering the Romanian stores that produce hand made fur coats and accessories as they are known for really good quality and longevity as well as stores that provide elegant men clothing.

19. Going Bowling Or Playing Pool

I very much enjoy playing bowling and pool, and the best place to do so is situtated near the train station, on Garii Boulevard.

Be aware the place is full with cool people and sometimes you might need to play a little bit of pool before being able to get to the bowling lane.

The atmosphere is relaxed and there are lots of tourists you can interact as well.

20. Visiting Museums

The History Museum, Art Museum and Urban Civilization Museum are surrounding Old Town. Visitation Hours start at 10 a.m. and close at 4 p.m., and can sometimes be closed for renovation, so make sure you check on their website the schedule for the precis time you're a tourist in Brasov.
The prices can start at 8 lei (2$) and may vary as sometimes in museum take place special events or charitable exhibitions.

21. Visiting The Old Walls Of The City

This is my favorite part of being in Brasov. The old walls of Brasov have easy access from Council Square, and also from the opposite part the Old Town. To get to the towers you just go up on the narrow streets that start at Council Square. Visiting those amazing towers is free of charge.

I enjoy visiting the walls and the towers.

22. Taking The Cable Car

Taking the cable car to the top of the mountain is one of the most relevant attractions in Brasov.

The price of a one way trip to the letters that spell Brasov is about 10 lei ($25) and the up/down ticket is 16 lei ($4).

Usually the is a line at all times, but it's worth it. The cable car has a capacity of twenty people so be ready to share some personal space.

23. Exercising

During summer time I prefer taking to route to letters that spell the name of Brasov, on foot. I usually get there in 30 minutes if I focus on my workout that combines exercises for all muscular groups, but other times can take a bit more especially when finding myself interacting with other tourists. Taking your way to Belvedere Platform by foot is a good cardio exercise.

24. Visiting Belvedere Platform

Belvedere platform is next to the letters that spell the name Brasov and from there you have the most beautiful view of the city, the near by mountains and the road to Poiana Brasov. You can take some amazing selfies.

If you're in mood for a cup of coffee or some juice, there is a small bar-store that provides coffee, water and soda but the prices are a bit high. They have a few tables, but it's not a cozy designed place to have a cup of coffee. I always make sure to have water with me and also a snack.

25. Visiting The Black Church

One of the most iconic structures in Romania is considered to be the token of Brasov. Visiting hours change based on time of the year and also church celebrations. The tourists can not attend the church service, but the magnificent organ can be heard from the Council Square. The Black Church is well known for it's architecture and black shadows left by the fire. I enjoy taking selfies there and also taking picture of the church from different places in the city as you can see it from any part of Brasov.

26. Hanging Out In Council Square

I love the atmosphere in Council Square. People are bounding, festivals can take part of your trip and there are always small independent boutiques where you can find hand made jewelry, traditional sweets made by citizens descending from saxons or szkely. Sometimes I admire the amazing fur coats they bring to the small market. I enjoy their traditional treats, bread and sweets.

27. Going To Poiana Brasov

I usually take the bus to Poiana Brasov. I really enjoy the view along the way and also the view from up there. The bus travels once every hour and the bus station is near to the City Hall.

The ticket price is the same with the one I use for moving across town, but the difference is that you need to buy this one from the bus station for Poiana Brasov and no other bus station.

Piana Brasov is well known for the winter sports and the great ski slope and hotels, but it's a great place to be during summer times as well.

I love going there in summer times and exploring the forest and have a bite to eat, a small pick nick.

28. Renting A Car

I don't rent a car in Brasov, because I like interacting with others and walking for site seeing. The prices start from 30 lei (8-9$) a day, and can go up depending on your preferences. Brasov is a place where everything interesting and fun is located at walking distance.

If you're interested in renting a car to go visit castles around Brasov, that could be one solution.

29. Parking Your Car

I'm not a fan of using the car in Brasov for good reasons and one of them is the parking space. The parking space is limited and you need to pay a subscription than can stat at one hour and can be weekly, monthly or for a longer period of time. Even if you pay a subscription, you're not guarantee the same parking space for your entire vacation. I consider the parking system to be a smart one, especially if you're being there for a long time or you need a car on daily bases.

30. Traveling To Places Near By

I take the minibus from the train station when I want to travel to castle Rasnov or castle Bran. The minibus can be 10-15 lei (2,5-3,5$) one way ticket and their schedule is pretty good starting at 9 a.m. to 6 p.m. with departures every 30 minutes. The taxi drivers might refuse to take you sightseeing. The reason for that is manly due to the fact they might need to come back without a costumer, and a one way drive does not cover the cost of petrol for coming back into town without a costumer.

When you say Brasov, you immediately think of Bran Castle or Moeciu, and of course Valea Prahovei that is just one hour away. Being in Brasov means taking the time to go to at least one of the places near by, like Castle Rasnov for example. Castle Rasnov is just 20 minutes away by car.

31. Getting To Know The City

Walking around the city without a map can be a great adventure, I adore the narrow streets that start from the Council Square, discovering the architecture and observing the contrast between buildings that have been renovated and the ones that start to degrade gracefully. There are a few empty unused hoses that are historical patrimony that can look a bit scary and that have written on a plaque a few things about their history. Use Google maps to find your way around the city and to find a certain place, as the app has been well adapted to every new change made by tourists or locals to improve the touristic guide.

32. Getting Inspired

Brasov is a great place to get inspired and old houses have a big role. With every journey I take, I find a new building that now is a historical patrimony but that looks a bit creepy and leads me to create stories about being hunted.

The Old Walls and Towers that have served as bastions in medieval times, are a good place to imagine what life was like during medieval times and help you imagine how day to day life was for people during those times.

33. Taking Pictures

I am passionate about photography and every single day is a challenge in Brasov. With lots iof tourist taking pictures non-stop I can be a bit distracted from my projects.

Beside all of this, there are loads of places that are great for taking great pictures. The Old Town is one o my favorite places to do so. I love the forest and connecting with nature. Every time I visit Brasov, I find myself taking pictures in the forest, or near by it. Taking pictures of plants, trees and houses in Brasov is one of my favorite things to do.

34. Speaking A Foreign Language

Brasov is known for the massive amounts of tourists, so speaking a foreign language is not a problem. The main language used with tourists is English, fallowed by German, Spanish and French. Asking for directions, a menu, advice or a drink will not be a problem.

Old people might be a bit reticent when speaking a foreign language, but young people are very open to conversation, polite and willing to help out.

35. Speaking Romanian

Locals appreciate it when they hear you using a few Romania words to show your respect and appreciation. Words like Buna ziua (Good afternoon), Buna seara (good evening), Multumesc (thank you) and Scuze (Sorry), are easy to learn and enough to know as a sign of gratitude. If you can't or won't keep in mind a few words, don't worry about it. No one will punish you for that. Don't worry about not being understood because even if locals seem a bit shy, they understand your needs.

36. Bounding With Locals

I find the locals to be very receptive to tourists. Besides, they are used to tourists in such way they have become a part of their life. Locals are pretty much open minded and kind. They like engaging into conversation and they are always polite. Most old people might not know English but they know German. Even so, they will be happy to hear you talking to them even if it is just to say Hello. Romanians love to have a good time and enjoy good sense of humor. If one of the persons I encounter is cold to me I don't insist in chatting when them, but if they are very much open to chatting I easily make friends.

37. Looking For An Adventure

Adventure Park Brasov is a great place to spend a few hours. The offer per person is 40 lei (10$) for three hours, having access to three difficulty levels. If one wants to spend more hour there will be a tax of 17 lei per hour, and a pass for the entire day is 800 lei. The park is at maximum capacity during summer time, and the routes for each level of difficulty are well designed to make you work it and also have fun. I like Adventure Park for what it offers: a good work out, good equipment and a chance to be in competition with others and test your abilities.

38. Swimming And Relaxation

Aqua Paradise is the place to be when outside is hot and you want to enjoy a full day if relaxation. Besides pools and slides, the facility offer massages and other spa services. Aqua gym is very popular and fun to do. Children also have a lot of fun. Prices may vary due to traffic or promotions and events they might have during summer time. I always enjoy a good massage in this facility.

39. Clubbing

Brasov is full of pubs and some of them are open until morning. Times pub is a cool place to spend time with friends, as well as Rasta Jamaica has a nice relaxed vibe.
If you are looking to party all night long you should try The Square located in Council Square.
You can find all kind of clubs around Brasov.
My suggestion is to read and search for pictures of them so you can get an idea about the club and decide if it's your style.

40. Getting Pampered

Women are known for the long hours they spend in from of mirrors before an event even if it's just a family dinner.
Brasov offers a variety of beauty salons for women and men, with easy access from Council Square, near hotels and inside shopping centers, as well as in the heart of all neighborhoods. The salons have decent prices and usually take cash.
I always make my appointment one day before in order to make sure they will have enough time to do my hair and avoid being in a hurry.

41. Singing Your Favorite Song

I love listening to live music and I consider karaoke live music. Although I'm not the one singing, I like going to Schwarz Pub and enjoy the atmosphere. The sound system is pretty good and they present us with a large variety of records to choose from. I have to admit that there are not the best of singer every time I am there, but even if they lack talent they can be a lot of fun as individuals. The place opens up at 9 p.m. and you usually don't need a reservation.

42. Skiing And Snowboarding

Poiana Brasov is the best place to practice winter sports. The ski slope here is one of the best in Romania. As for getting to the top of the ski slope, you can choose a pass for two or ten up travels, or you can choose a pass for the day/month.
The prices can differ from one year to another so make sure to check the prices on their website and at the gate.
Instructors can be booked but I suggest doing that in advance as the demand is high.

Winter gear can be bought all over Brasov and renting places usually are situated near the the ski slope. I recommend checking for an offer by hotel management or your hosts as they know the companies around Brasov and what they offer.

43. Listening To Live Music

In Brasov take place very year different festivals, usually during spring and summer time. The Council Square is the main festival location so make sure to book your trip a few months before in order to enjoy festivals like Oktoberfest or Cerbul de aur. Live music can be heard sometimes at Ciucas Tavern during summer times.

44. Drinking A Good Cup Of Coffee

Best coffee I ever had in Brasov was at Caffeol. They have a new concept that involves 400 ml jars of coffee mixtures and fruits or caramel. The regular coffee is very good as well, even if the prices might seem a bit high 10-36 lei (2.5-9.5$), you will enjoy the experience. In Council Square you can find Starbucks if you are not in the mood to try something different. The restaurants in Council Square have good coffee as well, but the frappes are cool, not awesome.

45. Having Treats

When I'm walking around Old town, I always find myself ending up on a bench in Council Square eating ice cream from the portable ice machine, or kurtos kolacs that are made on the spot. Kurtos kolacs are sweet and best to eat when warm. I love a well home made traditional treat especially because the ingredients are natural and organic.

46. Drinking Beer

I usually drin Ciucas when I'm in Brasov. I find it authentic being in the area Ciucas is made and it seems to taste batter there, than any other place. Pubs and restaurants, all have Ciucas and other Romanian beers or other companies like Heineken or Carlsberg. Artisanal beer can be found at local festivals.

47. Going To The Theatre

I very much enjoy the theater anywhere I am a tourist and have the chance to get a ticket, but Brasov Theater is unique. Over the years the director managed to get on stage best European actors, and the plays are usually directed by Romania directors that are well recognized over seas. Tickets must be bought at least three weeks before. Take this into consideration when booking a room and ask the hotel staff to buy the ticket or make a reservation for it.

48. Traveling By Train To Other Cities

When I book my trip, I always take into consideration visiting other cities like the ones on Valea Prahovei, or Sighisoara, Sibiu. It is best to buy the ticket one day before if you're traveling to Sibiu or Bucharest just to make sure you will have a seat.

If you leave exactly that day you can buy the ticket during the day, but be aware you might not have a seat.

You can travel by CFR (the Romanian company) or by RTF (private company) which is a bit cheaper and you can buy your ticket online without any worry.

49. Helping Others

There is one thing that disappoints me in Brasov, and that is
the appearance of beggars. I recommend avoiding them and
also the individuals that have a bag full of perfumes
especially when they start showing their abilities on speaking
multiple foreign languages.

On the other hand there are not going to be a problem due to
the fact that are just a couple of them and they are not
harassing anyone. I am more interested in charitable
organizations. I take the time to find out if there is any
charitable event taking place while I am there, because I
enjoy helping other, individuals that are in a different kind of
need.

50. Buying Souvenirs

I always buy souvenirs on my last day at Brasov. Republicii Street is full of shops where you can get hand made souvenirs, magnets for the fridge or key chans.

You can also find some leather goods at a really good price, although, keep in mind that those places take cash only.
A magnet is about 5 lei (4.25$) and the leather goods are estimated at 30-100 lei (6-25$).

Alexandra Florea

> TOURIST

GREATER THAN A TOURIST

Visit GreaterThanATourist.com
http://GreaterThanATourist.com

Sign up for the Greater Than a Tourist
Newsletter
http://eepurl.com/cxspyf

Follow us on Facebook:
https://www.facebook.com/GreaterThanATourist

Follow us on Pinterest:
http://pinterest.com/GreaterThanATourist

Follow us on Instagram:
http://Instagram.com/GreaterThanATourist

Alexandra Florea

> TOURIST

GREATER THAN A TOURIST

Please leave your honest review of this book on Amazon and Goodreads. Thank you.

We appreciate your positive and negative feedback as we try to provide tourist guidance in their next trip from a local.

> TOURIST

GREATER THAN A TOURIST

You can find Greater Than a Tourist books on Amazon.

Alexandra Florea

> TOURIST

GREATER THAN A TOURIST

WHERE WILL YOU TRAVEL TO NEXT?

Alexandra Florea

> TOURIST

GREATER THAN A TOURIST

Our Story

Traveling is a passion of this series creator. She studied abroad in college, and for their honeymoon Lisa and her husband toured Europe. During her travels to Malta, an older man leaving church tried to give Lisa some advice based on his own experience living on the island since he was a young boy. She thought he was just trying to sell her something. When traveling to some places Dr. Lisa Rusczyk was wary to talk to locals because she was afraid that they weren't being genuine. She created this book series to give you as a tourist an inside view on the place you are exploring and the ability to learn what locals would like to tell tourist. A topic that the writers are very passionate about.

Alexandra Florea

> TOURIST

GREATER THAN A TOURIST

Notes

Made in the USA
Monee, IL
14 November 2019